# DISCOVERIES IN PRAYER

Malachy Hanratty

# Discoveries in Prayer

the columba press

First published in 2007 by
the columba press
55A Spruce Avenue, Stillorgan Industrial Park,
Blackrock, Co Dublin


Cover by Bill Bolger
Origination by The Columba Press
Printed in Ireland by ColourBooks Ltd, Dublin

ISBN 978 1 85607 568 8

# Table of Contents

# Introduction

Did you ever think, 'I would like to be able to pray better'? Maybe this book will help.

Describing prayer as talking to God would satisfy most people. However, if I were to add to the definition '... and hearing God talking to me', I could expect many puzzled, or doubting, glances. Yet 'hearing' God is a deep, and very important, part of our praying. One aim of this book is to help develop this habit of listening.

The book is a summary of material that I gave, in many sessions, to various groups, over sixteen years. Each session consisted of a talk, a period of silent prayer, reflection on that prayer and sharing about it in small groups. These talks were allied to practising the contents in a step-by-step programme of about eighteen sessions. A printed summary of each talk was handed out after each session. This book is based on these handouts.

All this took place in Japan, where I have worked for over forty years in different parishes. Of course, the talks and printouts were in Japanese. Before I left, with the help of many participants I rushed to put the programme into book form. I wanted this, primarily, to help former participants start this programme for new groups in their own or other churches. Secondly, I wanted it as a help for participants continuing in groups that were carrying on without me. Lastly, I thought it might help the individual who picked up the book and wanted to experiment with the contents. I could imagine it being used as a do-it-yourself instruction manual.

But the bias of this material towards group use remains. I believe practising its suggestions in some kind of companionship with another or others has an added value.

It has since been suggested that I publish the talks in English. I have tried to adapt them for English speakers but it would be difficult for me to cut out the Japanese flavour and background.

Moreover, I have no experience of giving these talks outside Japan. So I can only ask the readers to make their own adaptations.

Because my Japanese vocabulary was not very extensive, I had to use simple, everyday language. I was also forced to search my own experiences and practices for concrete examples to explain what I had learned and discovered about prayer. However, in this kind of a book I regard that as an advantage rather than a deficit.

I called the programme 'Praying as a Human' in order to emphasise the place of the human faculties in opening us up to God's action, as well as aiming at as wide an audience as possible. Thus I don't advance into scripture or liturgy. However, I consider the basic elements of prayer which are presented in this book, to be a very important foundation for all kinds of prayer. Indeed, I made it a required preparation for subsequent courses on 'Praying Scripture' or 'Liturgical Prayer'.

I would like to think that anyone could find this programme helpful. The majority of the participants with whom I developed it were women with their families reared. Most of them had been baptised as adults, some others were not Catholic and still others were not baptised. Yet, out of this 'unexpected line up' some are now leading prayer-groups and some are even doing this with their fairly recently baptised husbands.

For this edition I acknowledge generous help from Columban Sisters and priests, the editors of the Columban *Far East* magazine, from family and many friends.

# CHAPTER ONE

## *The Good Things Prayer*

### Introduction

I have been doing this short prayer exercise daily for about 40 years. Among my different ways of praying I have found it the easiest, most appealing way for me. It has also had an amazing influence on all my other ways of praying. It has changed me in different ways. Some others who have tried this practice for some time, have claimed it changed their way of praying and also themselves in different ways.

More correctly, it should be called the 'The Daily Review of Good Things prayer-exercise', but let us just call it the Good Things Prayer. It is basically asking God to help me see more clearly some of the good things that he is continually giving me. I want to be able to notice them better. I find that the more I recognise them, the more I come to appreciate God's deep care of me in my daily life, and consequently I feel closer to God.

### What I mean by good things

When I say 'good things' here, I mean things like the following: things that during the day pleased me, made me happy, that gave me a positive feeling or attitude, that gave me energy.

Here are some examples:
* the joy of an unexpected meeting with someone I like very much;
* the delight of receiving a long-awaited letter;
* the satisfaction of something that turned out very successfully, e.g. a baked cake, a test, a difficult meeting, a business deal, an outing;
* the excitement of a fabulous bargain at the sale, getting the CD that I wanted;
* the relief over a worrisome problem solved;

* the relief and gratitude at finding a lost document;
* a refreshing walk on the shore, up a mountain, in a park;
* the warm feeling caused by someone being very kind to me, very patient with me and absolving my mistake;
* the delight and surprise at realising I was kind, patient, forgiving or gentle towards someone else;
* discovering a feeling of peace in myself, enthusiasm for some good work.

*How do I ask God to show me?*

Firstly I pick a short time. Each time, before starting, I decide for how long it will be, e.g. three minutes, or five, or, if I am very tired, only two – or whatever suits me at that time.

Then I put myself in as open, receptive and passive an attitude as possible and ask God, 'Show me some of the good things you gave me today.' I try to keep my mind empty. I resist thinking, searching or working to remember. I give the control to God. I want God to do all the work. The emphasis is on waiting for God to show me.

I find that repeating something like 'Show me, show me, show me,' or 'Show me good things, show me good things' helps keep me focused on waiting for God to do this work. Other people might not find this repetition helpful.

To me it is like sitting down before a TV screen and giving the remote control into God's hands. I then sit waiting patiently to see what he is going to show me. I try to discipline myself to wait till something pops into my mind. It reminds me of our old-time spring-toaster. I wait and wait and nothing seems to happen; then suddenly up springs the toast! So too I wait for a good thing to pop up. And often I am surprised.

*Wait! Wait! Wait!*

I suddenly realise that just waiting is very hard; it is not easy to keep one's hands off the remote control. I call this 'passive prayer'. As we follow this book and put it into practice, we will see how fruitful passive prayer is.

*Being surprised*

Often something unexpected pops up. When the something good happened during the day, it seemed a small thing and soon got lost in the crowded daily events. Now it shows itself as a much more important gift. I now feel the joy of it more consciously and strongly and often I can detect a message behind it.

I no longer expect things to show themselves in chronological order from the last time I did this exercise. It is usually the good things most strongly felt or the most recent good things that appear first. Indeed, I usually find that I am led backwards from the most recent good things to earlier ones. I think of it as 'reversing up' to the last review.

*A warning about the 'non-goods'*

Don't be surprised to discover that, when you make this special time to be quiet and wait to be shown good things by God, the first thing that enters your mind is the opposite. Let us call it a 'non-good'.

We seem to be so made that if, in a day, we had a hundred good things and only one or two non-goods, when we try to make a quiet space for ourselves, it would be the 'non-good' that would rush into that space and take over all our attention and feelings. It would not be the happy things but the unhappy memory of, for example, 'I scratched our new car today', or 'So-and-So slighted me today' or 'Oh, I neglected to phone …' causing a fierce urge in me to stop the prayer at once and go and phone before I forget again. I feel like I have to deliberately 'tighten my seat-belt' to keep myself from running away into activity.

For the first few months especially, we will experience this inclination to non-goods very often and very strongly. So, till we develop the practice better, we might have to spend most of the planned period just pushing out these non-goods. We tell them to wait at least till after the Good Things Prayer is over. When I suddenly realise that these non-goods have sucked me into themselves, I have to ignore them, and turn back to God asking, 'Are there no good things?' Then I must wait to be shown one.

Happily, as we develop this habit of praying, we will gradually find that good-things spring to mind much faster than before, and in greater variety. The non-goods should become less powerful in taking over the time.

### The value of non-goods

Later we will look at how to talk to God about these non-goods, too. They can be a valuable means for coming closer to God and other people. However, it is necessary to first meet God as a 'Giver of good things' before we can effectively talk to him about the non-goods.

### More explanations on the method

### When?

I do it every day at the time that suits best. It is usually before bedtime, but it can be done any time. For example, if you find you are usually too tired at bedtime, try noontime or before supper, or even at a different time every day if it suits you. But do it every day – even for a very brief time.

### Give the full time

It is important that you give the full length of time that you had decided on before starting, even if the whole time seems spent struggling with non-goods, or even if it looks like nothing will happen today. You will be surprised at times to find that it is in the last few seconds that something good jumps up, just like the toaster. Finish at the time decided.

### Place

This Good Things Prayer can be practised in all sorts of places, e.g. walking somewhere … waiting for a bus … working in the garden … ironing clothes … quietly warming oneself at the fire … in bed … in a warm bath, etc. Of course the less distractions the better. A quiet, calm, comfortable atmosphere is best.

*Try it and see*

When you first hear about the Good Things Prayer you might think it is too easy to be real prayer! I challenge you: try it and see.

I strongly suggest that you experiment and find the times and places and length of time that give you the best results. These differ according to each one's situation and character, and may have to change to suit changing conditions in one's life.

After some months, judge from any good changes in your prayer or in yourself, whether this prayer-exercise has any value for you.

*The following series*

This art of passive prayer is the foundation of the whole book, and as the daily Good Things Review is a good teacher of this art, make sure you spend time practising it before going on to longer exercises, which will be described in later chapters.

Also, after practising it faithfully for some months, Chapter 2 will be more easily understood.

In using this book with another person or with a group, it helps to read Chapters 13 and 14 now.

# CHAPTER TWO

# *About the Good Things Prayer*

*Is the good things exercise really prayer?*
When you first hear about this practice of the Good Things Prayer you might ask, 'Is this really prayer?' For many people, the word 'prayer' means saying certain special words learned from someone or somewhere else and said in certain circumstances. Usually it is said to obtain something from God or else with the feeling of fulfilling an obligation to God.

*Prayer is ...*
In this book the word 'prayer' has a much wider and deeper meaning. It means anything that makes our relation with God more conscious, intimate, deep, concrete. The effort is not so much trying to reach God as to increasing our awareness that God is trying to 'get through' to us, and we must switch on our receivers and respond more. That is what I mean by prayer. Listening and waiting and showing our inner selves to God are very important elements of prayer. Concentrating on God's activity is more important than paying all our attention to our own activity.

*Learning by discovery*
Learning by discovery gives deeper knowledge than just being told about something. When I was young, I was told by my elders that there was electricity in a live electric wire. I believed them, of course. Yet, out of curiosity, I deliberately touched a live wire. The shock I got went all the way to my ankles! I now knew in a different and deeper way what I had been told about electricity. Discovery by oneself reinforces our learning.

*Learning by doing*

If you have tried to learn to play the piano, swim, cook, drive a car or use a computer, you will know the importance of practice. Just hearing instructions or explanations is not sufficient.

Learning a good habit of prayer is no different. The purpose of this book is to help you learn by doing. This Chapter 2 will contain a lot of explanation. However, the following chapters will be about suggesting 'how to do' and encouraging you to 'try it and see what happens'.

*Difference between prayer exercises and a habit of prayer*

You have already experienced doing the Good Things Prayer. We call it a prayer exercise. It is very like putting in the time doing a physical exercise in order to become fit. The desired condition is to be fit all the time – not just when doing the exercise. The same holds with spiritual exercises. The goal is spiritual fitness, not just at the time of the exercise, but all the time. Hopefully, the exercises in this book will lead to spiritual fitness.

This spiritual condition will be shown by a growing habit that leads to 'praying always'. In this habit a person, more and more frequently, in all sorts of situations of daily life, turns to God spontaneously and with no plan. Prayer exercises develop, maintain and deepen this habit.

*The 'Good Things Prayer' is a prayer exercise*

As you see, the Good Things Prayer is a prayer exercise – a very special and foundational prayer exercise. It helps us to do other kinds of prayer better and, especially, it teaches the 'passive prayer' that is necessary to do longer prayer-exercises.

We can call it the *backbone* of this series of prayer exercises. We can't emphasise enough how important it is to do it every day, even for a very short time.

*Longer prayer exercises*

In the following chapters I will suggest longer prayer exercises.

These require at least 15 minutes. I suggest you do them as often as you can – maybe once or twice a week in the beginning. Hopefully, as you begin to find fruit and strength coming from them, it will get easier to find time and desire to pray these more often and to lengthen them.

If the daily Good Things Prayer could be called the *backbone* of this effort to obtain a 'habit of prayer', these longer exercises can be called the *muscles*. They add strength and growth to 'spiritual fitness'.

### Try and see what best suits you

I suggest that you seriously try each long exercise for a while and discover if any of them help you. Trying an exercise only two or three times is not enough. After trying different exercises for some time, concentrate on those two or three exercises that are most fruitful, and use them often.

Everyone is different. Just as each one wears different clothes, so each one finds that certain ways of praying and certain prayer exercises suit him or her best. You can also find that the choice of different times of the day, different lengths of the exercises or different places, can better prepare you for fruit from the prayer. These 'best conditions', of course, may change as we ourselves change.

### 'Judge from the Fruit' is the test of usefulness

We judge the effectiveness of these exercises from their results. After praying in this way for some time – at least three or four months – do we notice any change in ourselves? For example, do these exercises help us to see things in a new light? Are we becoming more thankful people? Or more generous or patient or even more relaxed and trusting? Are we more aware of God at work in the 'ups and downs' of our daily lives? And later, have we realised that God was with us in both our joys and our sorrows, in our successes and failures, in our strengths and weaknesses? This is how we judge the value of these exercises.

### Reviewing
Reviewing one's prayer time, as shown above, can be very valuable and will be explained more fully in Chapter 6.

### Sharing
The value of sharing about prayer with another person, or others, is taken up in Chapter 13.

### Who can use the good things exercise?
In Japan some of the participants of these courses, as Sunday-school teachers, used the Good Things Prayer exercise for primary-school children with good results. I also taught these exercises to over-seventies and some have used them amazingly well. Many of the participants had been finding their old way of praying had become dull, listless and was not giving any strength to face the challenges of daily life. For them these exercises were a new step into deeper prayer and coming closer to God. As long as there is a desire to pray better, and at the same time a willingness to give time and effort to discovering how, this book should help.

### Praying as a human
As I said in the Introduction, I don't use liturgy or scripture in this book. I limit myself to fundamental elements which are in prayer of any kind. These are:
* turning to a Greater Power that is outside ourselves.
* believing this Greater Power works in everyone's life to bring all closer to Itself and to one another.
* involving the basic elements of prayer that I have emphasised above – waiting passively, noticing, responding. Thus, here I speak only about praying using the human faculties.

However, these basic elements of prayer are fundamental to Christian prayer in all its forms. This becomes evident as we move into liturgical prayer or praying with scripture.

*More uses of the good things exercise*

This way of praying can be used as a preparation for meetings or before a family meal or such. All together can use two or three minutes in silence to look at their good things since the last meeting, family meal, etc.

On a personal note, I often use it as a preparation for Mass, or for the Sacrament of Reconciliation, etc.

*Putting your petition 'on hold'*

If you pick up this book looking for help to get a problem solved, a suffering taken away, help in a relationship or such, for a while put your desire on 'hold' or in 'a bottom drawer'. Spend time and effort, through these early exercises, to get to know God better and discover his wanting to care for you. Then you can open the drawer and, together with God, look at the problem.

*Group use of this book*

Experience has shown that where people join together in some way to try to improve their prayer life, prayer itself becomes deeper and often easier. Chapter 14, *For Groups*, develops this theme and throughout the book I will, occasionally, give hints on group use.

*The spiritual journey*

Each one of us is on a journey. It is a journey in which God is always inviting us into a greater closeness to himself which, in turn, leads to a greater closeness to one another. God is inviting us to discover that he is always with us. He is inviting us to listen to him and to talk to him. This is what prayer does for us. But I hope this book will help you discover these things for yourself.

# CHAPTER THREE

# A Longer Good Things Prayer

Here is another exercise that develops the habit or art of praying. It is based on the daily good things review. Both exercises focus on God's activity, asking God to show us some of the good things that he is doing in our lives.

However it differs in that:

* the prayer period is longer.
* the chosen period for seeing good things is longer.

*How I do this Exercise*

* Each time, my first step is to decide for how many minutes I am going to do it, but I learned from experience that I need at least 15 minutes to 'get into' it.
* My second step is picking a period of my life longer than one day to look at. For example, during this last month, a certain year, on a recent holiday or since some important event in my life, since the change in my life situation, since meeting some new person or joining a new group.
* Then my third step is asking God to show me some of the good things I have received during this time. As in the daily Good Things Prayer, I try to relax and wait passively to see what comes up.

I myself usually start by slowly repeating silently the same word or phrase over and over again. I usually say, 'Please show me, Please show me,' or something like that. This helps me to keep focused on God at work and on my own desire to see good things.

*Not hurrying on*

When something pops up, I stay looking at it as long as I can. It might even surprise me because I hadn't adverted to it till now. Then I notice the warm, happy feelings this gives me. I might discover myself repeating 'that was good, that was good'. Then I might notice myhead wanting to actively search for a bigger example of the one that popped up. I have to resist this urge. I try to stay with this small example and try to taste more fully the good feelings it has given. I stay with it till another good thing pops into the centre of my awareness or memory and takes over my attention.

### No order of appearance

Like the short daily Good Things Prayer, I often find myself reversing-up from very recent things to things at the beginning of the period being covered. For the most part, very recent good things appear first. At other times, some big or strong event during the period comes to mind first.

### Feelings

The aim is not to make a list of good things, but rather to notice and taste the good feelings that they cause in me and notice how this affects me positively. Later, I realise that fruitful changes in me flow from these effects.

### Distractions

If I discover myself 'distracted', I go back to the start and ask again to be shown. For example, I suddenly find myself planning a holiday, thinking about getting a new computer or how to hit a better shot at my favourite game. Then I realise that these things have taken over all my attention. So I have to go back to the start and ask God again to show me, show me, show me what he has already given me during this longer period of my life.

### Dealing with non-goods

Sometimes, like in the daily good things exercise, I might notice that a non-good has taken control of my attention. For example, some worry or anger or fear has taken up all my thoughts and feelings and energy. So I turn to God and start asking 'Show me a good thing'. I stay like this till my planned time is up.

*Being shown good things in non-goods*
I emphasise again: don't get sucked into a non-good. Keep putting it outside this prayer exercise time and keep asking to be shown some good thing. In longer exercises there may be occasions when it seems to be impossible to keep these 'non-goods' out of the prayer. So, after trying hard for a long time to keep them outside the prayer time, I change my asking. I turn to God and start asking, 'In this suffering is there not one little good thing? Show me that!' I find that if I keep asking like this, eventually something will pop up and then I stay with that good thing.

*Full time*
Why should we decide a time-length, and why always try to use the full time? Many people have had the following experience. Sometimes nothing seems to be happening during the prayer time. It just seems hopeless and feels tiresome and frustrating. So they want to give up on that prayer time, but instead, they doggedly keep trying for the full length of time. And it is in the last few seconds that something amazingly pops up. After you have had a few delightful experiences like that, you begin to understand why waiting out the full time is so important.

Also you will know, from your experience of training for physical fitness, how helpful it is to use a decided length of time for a particular physical exercise. It is the same for these exercises for spiritual fitness.

*More examples of longer good things exercises*
Here are more examples of periods in my history that I pray. This list may start you finding periods like these in your own life. After some time you will discover what periods are most fruitful for you in your present spiritual condition:

* during the previous month,
* during my recent trip,
* when I was in secondary school,
* when I was in the ... football team,
* since I started working at ...,
* since I got married,
* since I moved to ...,
* since I met ...,
* since I joined the music group,
* (a special one), since I started the Good Things Prayer.

*A two-week challenge*

Here is a special challenge to help you understand this exercise. For at least 15 minutes each day for a week, pick a different period in your life and ask to be shown good things during that time. Notice, or better still write down, the good things that you have discovered and how this makes you feel.

Then the following week, do the same periods over again and notice how different things come up. Repeating the same exercise, different fruit! I use the word fruit to indicate particular benefits which may result from a period of prayer.

This means that the same periods can be used again and again because each prayer period will be a new experience with different fruit. Repeating gives an idea of the wide possibilities and riches in this exercise. Indeed, I recommend repeating periods, hoping to find more fruit in each. Then I suggest that you pick two or three of the most fruitful periods and use them often. As we return to the various periods we become more and more aware of the constancy of God's presence and his care for each one of us.

Periodically reviewing one's notes can be very fruitful

*Fruit*

By fruit I mean both good things that pop up and the good effects they cause in me. At the beginning, material objects or concrete items will be the big part of the things noticed. But later more internal and less visible things will start to appear. For example, I may someday realise the patience of another towards me and then, some later day, I will notice – to my surprise – a new patience in myself towards someone else. I now realise that it too was a good thing; and indeed, a bigger good thing. However, it is important to know that it takes quite some time practising this exercise before I become aware of deeper realisations like this. We must be patient with ourselves. After all, God is!

*The daily good things review always a must*
I recommend all these longer exercises *in addition to* the daily good things review. I firmly believe that the daily review is the backbone of our growth in prayer. It should never be neglected, no matter how short it may be. Then these longer ones can build up the muscles.

# CHAPTER FOUR

# Finding Messages from God in my own History

*Discovering God at work in surprising coincidences*
This prayer-exercise helps me to 'hear' messages from God that influence me now. Through being shown again certain coincidental events of my own history, I learn more about God's attitude to me. I discovered this exercise in the following way.

One morning when I was doing a longer Good Things Prayer in my parish in Japan, the memory which I will relate below popped up. I got a lot of fruit from it. It gave me a message from God and affected my daily living when I repeated the prayer. As I wanted to see more of these coincidences in my life, to hear the messages and be influenced by them, I developed this new exercise.

As you will see, I do it in the same way as I do the longer Good Things Prayer exercise. That means that, in a decided period of time, I ask God to show me again certain things that have a message for me and I wait passively, with expectation and patience, for something to pop up. These special things are co-incidental events of my life that teach me about God's attitude to me. Also they show me certain incidents that led me to be here at this time and able to pray like this. The following is the memory that came up during that longer Good Things Prayer.

*The incident*
I was brought back to an experience I had the last time I was home on holidays in Ireland. Late one night, far from home, my car broke down. I was told where a mechanic lived. So reluctantly and diffidently, I went along to ask his help. To my amazement he knew me and gave me a great welcome. He was from my home town. He had been a few classes below me in the same primary school and remembered me well. He was delighted to

help. He went out to fix my car and his wife even made a tasty supper for me while I was waiting. And he refused any payment, saying, 'The next time you are in the area, call in.' I came away so delighted and grateful. I was amazed how good God had been to me. He even changed what was a hardship into a joy.

Then I realised in my prayer of that morning the further truth. And I said to God, 'It is amazing to think that over forty years beforehand, you made preparations to look after me that night.'

*How I do this exercise*
I do this prayer-exercise in the same way as I do the Good Things Prayer exercise. That means I ask:
* to be shown more clearly coincidences that influenced the path leading to my present condition,
* to understand more deeply the messages they give me,
* that I allow these messages to influence me now.

*I decide for how long*
Each time I decide for how long I am going to do the exercise and I resolve to stick to the chosen time. For example, as I begin to learn how to do this, I will pick at least 20 minutes.

*I wait to be shown*
Then, repeating slowly and rhythmically 'Show me how you led me to this place,' I wait to see what comes up. And the waiting becomes the important thing.

As I said, I find in my passive prayer that the repetition of a word or a phrase helps me to stay focused while waiting, to see things in a new way and to notice my changing feelings. The word or phrase may keep changing too as I notice what is happening inside me. Of course, this happens in various ways from person to person because God leads each one individually.

*Results*

I have done this exercise often and each time what I am shown, or the way I am shown it, or what strikes most strongly, is different and unexpected. Sometimes I see many things; other times I am caught by just one or two significant experiences; sometimes I have to patiently wait through dark periods when nothing happens. Sometimes an amazing coincidence pops up. One example was, walking across a busy intersection, I unexpectedly met someone I had badly wanted to meet but couldn't contact, yet, here to my joy, was that person, smiling at me. Yet, if I had come 30 seconds earlier or 30 seconds later I would have missed that person completely.

Ultimately, this says to me that Someone looks after me. Sometimes it is during the prayer itself that I become aware of this message; sometimes it is in the review after the prayer that I realise it.

*The jig-saw's message*

When I notice two or three of these amazing coincidences occurring close together and connecting to form a big clear picture, I am reminded of a jig-saw puzzle. It gives me a message that some Great Power outside myself is putting things together for me and saying, 'You are important to me!'

*Noticing such coincidences outside prayer periods*

For me, doing this exercise from time to time has led to a spontaneous habit, outside a prayer exercise, of quickly noticing 'The Jig-saw Maker' working in my daily living. I now more quickly notice this when these things happen. For example, in happy meetings on escalators, trains, at airports, I suddenly recall that the 'Great Planner' is at work.

I am into retirement age, yet I can still notice, for example, how a childhood hobby can be a source of help to me even now. Or I find people whom I had met many, many years before, now come back into my life to play a different role. Even people I once quarrelled with have since become close friends.

*Later fruit from painful experiences*

Even the experience I have obtained through painful events, dark miserable periods, even mistakes or embarrassments, has become very useful now for myself or for others. When I notice this I have to say, 'You were with me then and I didn't notice it', or 'You were preparing then to help me *now*.'

*More personal experiences*

As I see myself now, an old Japanese missionary, I want to smile. I remember well the night, a month after ordination as a Columban missionary priest, that our superior gathered us together to tell us what missionary country we had been appointed to. I had a few favourite mission countries in mind but Japan was not one of them. It was said the language was very difficult, took endless study that, at best, gave poor results. There were all kinds of rules of etiquette, and for a young idealistic missionary 'adventurer' it was like being put into a straightjacket. It was said it was really difficult to get to know anyone there. And after all this, there were few results for one's efforts. But, to my disappointment, I was sent to Japan. And for the first 20 years or so I felt all these things very much.

But gradually things changed. Now, half a century since that night when I was appointed, I can look back and say, 'I am so grateful that I was sent to Japan. I don't think I would have developed the way I did somewhere else.' I wonder would I be as contented or energetic as I am now. I doubt it! I certainly changed continually during the years. And as I changed, I discovered that Japanese people seemed to change at the same time. And it was then I discovered that I could really get to know people deeply. Yes, Japan was the best place for me to be sent to. It shows that God is smarter than I am!

*Prayer exercise review*

For about five or six minutes I review what happened. Here are examples of questions that I ask myself. I don't use them all each time.

What did I get from the prayer time; do I feel different now compared to the start of my prayer?

Were there any surprises: e.g. in seeing a new connection between people or events almost forgotten or any amazing coincidences?

What feelings did these give rise to?

Did I get any message?

How well did I wait?

Would I like to do this exercise again?

Is there anything I would like to write in my notebook or tell another about?'

*Suggestion*

Do the above ' history' exercise a number of times. Try some reviewing. Use a notebook.

# CHAPTER FIVE

# Meeting God in Nature

*Praying and not realising it*

There are some people who pray, yet do not realise that what they are doing is praying. 'Praying Nature' can be one good example of this. But I think I can best explain this by first telling a story.

*A story*

Some years ago when I was teaching this series, I asked some of those attending it to help me in talking about nature as a help to prayer. I regarded them as more in contact with nature than myself. I asked them to speak out of their own relationship to nature, and about any help it gave for praying or feeling closer to God and experiencing change. One lady was a very talented but shy and retiring person. But here is what I remember of her talk. It certainly impressed and helped me. I will try to give it in her words.

*The flower spoke to her*

When Father teased me again that the time had come to give a talk to this group about my experiences with nature, this time I didn't hesitate, even for a moment, in saying 'Yes'. Previously I would have said 'No' instantly. When I was asked this time, I felt something inside me saying 'The time has come!' So I accepted Father's request without hesitation!

I believe that my attitude towards life has changed dramatically since I spent time gazing at the wonder of a wild flower blooming quietly by itself on the roadside. It is called a 'skullcap'. I have seen them growing in bunches in the woods and on the river banks. But I had never seen a lone one, blooming on a busy roadside, and growing up through thick concrete. I gazed at that flower for a long, long time, wondering where did this frail looking little flower get the marvellous power to patiently force its way up through that hard concrete to bloom in the light.

Then I realised that I was, till now, exactly like a usual 'skullcap', growing in a cosy and safe place in the middle of a bunch and not trying to do anything special. However, through this little flower I was being shown that God had sown certain strengths in me too a long time ago and now the time had come for me to display the gifts I had received. I felt a great desire to break through my own hard shell and to come out, to bloom and display the fruit of the Spirit. And since that time, although it is rather slow, I find myself changing in different ways.

*Our present day relationship with nature*
We don't have to go to Niagara Falls, the Sahara desert, the Grand Canyon or the Himalayas to be enthralled by nature. To stand on high cliffs gazing, awestruck, at gigantic North Atlantic waves or, meditatively, at an evening ring of purple mountains, is to experience being drawn deeper into oneself and closer to nature. Sadly, we soon forget its influence as we go our busy tourist way.

We are far removed from working with the soil or with animals or trees or growing the food we eat. We would not think of spending a quiet day alone in a little boat just listening to nature. I once climbed Mt Fuji – surrounded by the noise of the loud radios people carried with them! Of course we leave offices in groups to go off and view the cherry-blossoms, but don't think of hearing any message from them. Usually I eat my food in a hurry, almost without tasting it. If alone, I feel I should be reading the newspaper at the same time. I don't try to let the taste talk to me.

Today we live in a world surrounded by so much that is manufactured by ourselves. It is a world of concrete, steel and plastic. We are surrounded by the noise of engines, loudspeakers and traffic. We smell smog and chemicals and exhaust fumes. This is the air we breathe.

We can see a beautiful sunset or rainbow, a cat playing with her kittens, or hear birds singing in a forest and smile and hurry on and quickly forget. We don't make time to let these touch us inside. Giving a glance and a nod at Mt Fuji from the Bullet Train is a good metaphor of our modern relationship to nature.

Yet, deep within us we know how it can influence us. Just think of the different ways a dull dreary day in February or a bright blue sky in April, can influence us. After a day hiking in the mountains, after a long walk through the fields or even after an hour weeding in the garden, we are different people. So these thoughts urge us to devote time to coming closer to nature.

We can do this for recreation, for example, walks on an autumn leaf-strewn path, along a sandy shore or a shaded river. Or we can be attentive to nature as an open door to inner stillness and peace. We are drawn into prayer.

Here is what I call 'Praying Nature.' I will summarise the steps, then explain them in more detail.

*How to 'pray nature'*
1. Pick an object in nature to focus on.
2. Decide how long you will give to the exercise, then adhere to it.
3. Concentrate only on intently gazing at (or hearing, smelling, feeling or tasting) the object. Be passive. Let the object draw you closer to itself.
4. Notice what is gradually happening inside yourself. Notice how you want to respond.

*Picking an object*
Here are some examples. They involve using the senses of sight, sound, smell, touch, taste or inner senses of imagination or memory:

Gazing steadily at a flower, a potted plant, a butterfly in the garden, the moon on a frosty night, a sunset, snow falling,

the first green shoots breaking through the winter soil, a bird gathering materials for her nest, ants busily working together.
*Listening* to waves on the shore, the gurgling of a stream, birds singing on a spring morning, the wind in the trees.
*Smelling* newly mown grass, wood-smoke, roses.
*Feeling* a soft, fresh breeze on your face, the warm sun on your neck, the heat of a cosy fire, a new woollen sweater.
*Tasting* slowly each mouthful of food, cool spring water on a hot day, freshly picked strawberries, red wine.

### Indoors

We can still pray this way indoors by staring out a window at scenery, at a garden, a bird. Some people pray while listening to tapes of birds singing and other nature sounds; other people burn candles that emit aromas of flowers; still others may use a picture of lovely scenery, of a pet, a flower arrangement.

In a quiet place we can use our *imagination* or *memory* to enter nature. We can imagine ourselves as being an oak tree, a snowflake, a canary, a violet, a river, a dog.

Or we can remember a special scenic view, or a mountain climb.

Experiment with different objects, using different senses. Find your own favourite objects that touch and affect you best and find which sense is easiest for you to use. Then pray these favourites frequently.

### Deciding the length of the prayer

Each time, first decide the length of the prayer time and use it fully. I recommend at least 20 minutes.

### Prayer time

Begin by just concentrating on gazing steadily at (listening to, feeling, smelling or tasting) the chosen object. At the beginning you may even find it very hard to hold your gaze like this for five minutes. But this struggle to resist thinking, judging, reflecting or doing 'something else' is a sign that you are on the right track. You must be passive; keep your mind empty. You must just wait to see what happens.

Gradually we will discover, more and more, details that we had not noticed before. These draw us closer and closer to the object. We might even imagine this object of nature 'talking' to us. Or we might find ourselves having a conversation with the object.

One lady shared about being deep in the mountains and feeling 'Silence so deep it seemed to hug me with strong arms'. Once while gazing at angry waves crashing on rocks, I seemed to hear them say, 'You are not alone, we know your frustration'. Realisation comes: God is whispering to us in such moments.

### Results: Inner changes
These experiences of being drawn closer can give us new strength. The experience of the lady in our opening story of the little skullcap flower is a perfect example of praying nature, and praying spontaneously too.

### Frightening side of nature
Of course, there are negative reactions from experiences of nature, e.g. in thunder and lightning, earthquakes, hurricanes, volcanoes, floods, etc. We will want to learn how to pray through these negative experiences too. However, following this book, get used to praying through the positives first. Then we can learn how to discover values in the negatives also.

# CHAPTER SIX

# Reviewing Prayer Exercises and Ways of Praying

I was surprised when at a prayer workshop it was suggested that we review our prayer exercises. However, as I followed through on the suggestion and experienced positive results from it, I made reviewing a practice which I now rarely omit. Here I wish to explain what review of prayer is and how I approach it.

The first thing to note is that reviewing prayer is different from prayer itself. In prayer – especially passive prayer – thinking can be an obstacle; in reviewing, thinking is essential. Thinking is, as it were, talking to oneself; prayer is talking and, more importantly, listening to God. We will look now at:

1) review of a prayer exercise just finished and
2) review of habits of praying over a period of time.

## I. REVIEWING A PRAYER EXERCISE JUST FINISHED

*For a short time*
I am thinking of a review of about five minutes of prayer exercises of over twenty minutes duration.

*Soon after each prayer exercise*
I say 'soon after', because if it is too long afterwards, some things will not be remembered clearly enough. Yet, it is a good thing to have some kind of a break between the prayer and the review; it might only be a change of place or posture or, perhaps, relaxing over a cup of tea.

*Examining what happened during the prayer time*
In reviewing, I ask myself questions like the ones below. Of course, I do not ask all these questions each time. The important ones seem to come up spontaneously if I make the time and con-

centrate. These are only examples to help each one discover his or her own best questions.

### How did the prayer finish up?

This, for me, is usually the most important question. I ask myself how I was feeling at the end of the prayer. Then, briefly I think back to the beginning. This helps me to notice any changes that happened during it. Firstly, I focus on positive feelings or new ways of seeing things or on a new energy in myself. 'What fruit did I get out of this prayer?' is another way of asking this question. When I notice negative things, I ask myself 'What are these telling me?'

### Did the time go fast?

I find this question useful. Generally speaking, a prayer time that passes quickly was focused. I may have had to struggle a lot. Perhaps I may have had to go back to the beginning many times and ask again for what I was praying. It may even have been a painful exercise but I was there – attentive and alert.

### Did I finish up feeling drawn to respond in some way?

When a prayer time is energetic, I find it often follows the following steps. Firstly, I notice that I am beginning to see something in a new way. Then, I notice this has caused new feelings in me. From these new feelings come new desires and new energy and I may feel drawn to a new response. For example, I am praying for someone who has hurt me. Then something pops into my mind that might make me see this person in a new light, perhaps how he or she may have been hurt in his or her own history. I now find this is beginning to give me compassion, and a desire to understand this person more.

### Do I want to do this prayer exercise again?

I often feel that I must repeat this prayer – maybe many times. Sometimes it is because it was a busy, fruitful prayer and I finished up strengthened, grateful, determined or challenged. At other times, I might feel that there was something important to receive from this prayer but that I really hadn't yet received it. So I would want to go back to listen again.

*Has a special summarising word or symbol or feeling popped up?*
Occasionally, a special word or symbol that summarises wonderfully the fruit of the prayer, pops up. Then I find that, if during my daily living I recall that word or symbol, much of the feeling and fruit of the prayer is renewed in me.

*Is there anything about this prayer that I would like to share with someone?*
Good sharing comes out of good reviewing.

*Conclusion*
It is evident that reviewing holds many benefits. It deepens awareness of what happens in prayer. It sharpens the call to respond. Sometimes in prayer itself it may seem that God is not present but in the review some particular thing, unexpected and unnoticed till now, shows he is there, hearing and answering.

### II. REVIEWING AFTER A LONGER PERIOD
### OF PRACTISING PRAYER EXERCISES

*Periodic review*
After a certain period of time, I look back over my habits of praying. For example, I might decide to do it on the last Sunday of each month for about 20 minutes or so. I always do it during my retreats. In a prayer group, a special time for this review can be scheduled.

I ask myself questions like the following:
*Am I giving the full time?*
I check to see how well did I wait till the end of the full time.

*What seemed to be the best time of the day for me?*
Some people pray best early in the morning; some pray best at night. Some people do best by having a fixed time each day;

others find changing the time to suit circumstances gives them the best results. So each person might ask, 'What time usually helps me best?' One of the strongest suggestions in this book applies here: experiment and discover.

*What is the best length of time for me?*
This likewise is to be discovered by experimenting with different lengths of time.

*Am I finding and using the best places?*
Where I pray has an influence on my prayer. Quiet is always an advantage; noise a distraction or obstacle. Comfort too is important. If I am praying in a place too warm or too cold, or in an uncomfortable position, I cannot pray as well as in a comfortable place or position. The experimenter will learn these from experience. Also, for example, sleepy experiences teach me that after a big, heavy meal, sitting in a warm, comfortable place, it will be hard to have a very deep, concentrated, fruitful prayer!

*Am I, since I started following this method of prayer, discovering anything about God? About myself? About my relation to God? About praying?*

*Have I ever been surprised at what I discovered during these exercises or prayers?*

*Am I finding favourite exercises?*

*Am I growing or deepening in any way?'*

*Reviewing is a natural practice*
I said in the beginning that I was surprised to hear there was such a thing as reviewing prayer and that it was a very valuable practice. But now I realise I should not have been surprised. After all, it is a very natural thing to want to discover what caused something to go well so it might be repeated or to find what hindered something from going well.

The housewife who is delighted with what she has just baked, may unconsciously review her efforts. She might ponder, 'Was it that new brand of flour, was it that particular oven temperature or was it the different baking time that gave this better result?' Or after hitting a good shot at his favourite sport or even more so, after having hit a bad one, the player starts thinking 'maybe I should try doing ...' etc. So when one wants to improve, spending time noticing what went well, or what did not, or what might improve things, is not so strange.

OTHER HELPS

### Body stillness

When my mind is very busy and 'jumpy' with many things, I find that walking slowly can use up some of the unnecessary energy, and help keep me calm and waiting. But I notice that when something deep catches me, I spontaneously pause or stop. This proves that naturally a still body is best for deep passive prayer.

### Breathing

Normally, I do not consciously use breathing-exercises to help my prayer, but many people do.

### Using a notebook

Using a notebook for jotting down important points from review can be valuable. In fact this book on prayer has been born from piles of notes made after reviews of my prayer.

### Patience

It takes some people a long time to learn how to review and get something out of it. So be patient with yourself. Fruit will eventually appear if you persevere.

*Putting into practice*

'Am I putting into practice what we have studied so far?' is a question to ask oneself continually, as you use this book. The chapters here are not just to teach. It is no good if one reads them and says 'Now I am delighted to understand that,' and does not start practising them very, very often – if not daily. Rushing off to the next chapter, without trying to put the previous one into practice, really doesn't help growth in prayer at all. Some practice and God's help will show when to move on.

This is something for leaders of prayer groups to remember to emphasise.

# CHAPTER SEVEN

# Meeting My Own God

Here, I want to share with you the most important discovery I made through practising the Good Things Prayer. I will explain how valuable this discovery is for growth in prayer.

*What I discovered*
After practising this prayer for some time, I noticed that as I waited passively, and then became aware of good things popping up on my inner 'TV screen', I also noticed feelings of surprise, gratitude or joy that came with them. Then, later, I noticed that I would be repeating silently, rhythmically, in awe, words like 'You were there!' or 'You were at work there!' or 'You are good to me!' or words like that, while being conscious of God's presence.

*A mantra*
Later I learned that this rhythmic repetition which I had experienced is used by many peoples in their practice of passive or contemplative prayer, to keep the mind from wandering in different directions and to keep it focused on what it is waiting for. It is often called a *mantra*, which is a word from Sanskrit, meaning an instrument of thought. It is much used by Buddhists, Hindus and others. I found it coming naturally to me and helping me to concentrate.

*My own mantra*
So what had been happening to me was that I was discovering mantras of my own that helped me to encapsulate what I was experiencing concerning God's contact with me. Gradually, one of these, 'You are at work!' became my mantra. I noticed too, I would spontaneously say it in different ways; sometimes em-

phasising the word 'You', at other times the words 'at work'. Of course, it contains many of the meanings of the other mantras too, such as God being 'with me', 'being good to me', etc.

### Find your own mantra

Those drawn to praying with a mantra, will probably experience it revealing itself progressively. In the beginning, it is usual to find more than one. However, gradually a particular one will emerge as the No 1 favourite. This is to be accepted, with gratitude, as one's own personal mantra. Perhaps later it may change, due to new experiences in prayer or a different situation in life, or an older mantra may come back but with more strength. Prayer review can be very helpful in discovering the mantra.

### Using that discovery – in reverse

### Using my mantra or 'prayer-mobile' to contact God

An even more important discovery I made was that I could use my own mantra in reverse. I found that, when I didn't feel in contact with God, by deliberately beginning to repeat my mantra, I could be brought back into contact with God again. I was being brought back to where I had previously felt I had met God. Just as I discovered that the new feelings of contact gave rise to my mantra, I also discovered that repetition of the mantra could give rise to feelings of contact with God.

I learned to use this at the beginning of all kinds of prayers or during prayer if, for example, I became distracted, to bring myself into contact with 'my own God' again. Sometimes I call this my 'prayer-mobilephone' rather than 'my mantra.'

### My own God

When I say 'my own God', I am thinking of a God that is more than the God I have been told about by others. It is the God I have met in experiences in my daily life and a God who shows me that I am important to him. He looks after me and I feel he wants to draw me closer. That's what I mean by 'my own God.'

## Calling myself up

Of course this prayer-mobile is really not to call God up. It is to call myself up! I call myself back before the God I met before. I am calling myself out of all the clutter and obstacles that are overcoming me, and keeping me from seeing God at work here. My head tells me that God is always there waiting for me; it is I who have wandered off out of contact. God never switches off his mobile phone! He is always gently trying to whisper to me. I often forget to switch mine on. So my own mantra is like my own prayer-mobile number which God has given me for quick contact. Imagine God, in my prayer, showing me that private prayer-mobile number which he has prepared for me for better contact.

## Times I deliberately use my mantra

### To start my prayer

I have discovered that my mantra is a great way to start praying, especially when I am tired, upset, distracted, scattered, angry, etc. It clears away confusing thoughts, tidies up scattered feelings and creates space for me to turn to face God. It is like someone who helps me tidy up my room to receive a visitor.

Also, when I am vague about *whom* I am really trying to talk with during the coming prayer time, it helps me to focus and brings me into contact with God.

### If distracted during prayer time

Also during my prayer time, if I notice I have wandered off from contact and got lost in thinking or distractions, this mantra can help bring me back into contact with God again. I 'dial in'; that is I deliberately start repeating my mantra.

### I use this practice before all kinds of prayer

So now, I usually use this practice for starting all kinds of prayers, e.g. preparation for Mass or for the Sacrament of Reconciliation. No doubt the reader can easily understand how this practice helps before a prayer of thanks or of praise, but will probably be surprised to hear how important it is before a prayer of petition.

It may cause even more surprise when I say that I use my mantra at the beginning of angry and complaining prayers. I will talk about these kinds of prayer later.

But the big point I want to emphasise here is that, before asking God for things, or before we can tell God how we are feeling, or before we can listen to him, we first have to be in contact with him. We first have to put ourselves before our own God. This prayer-mobile, switched on, is my way for contacting him.

### Throughout my day

Till now I have been talking about prayer exercises and scheduled times of prayer. But I am also discovering that this habit causes the mantra to spontaneously arise during different activities and happenings of my daily life. If something joyous and unexpected happens I may find it springing up. I find myself repeating silently and almost unconsciously, 'You are at work.' At other times, when I am in a happy or reflective mood, I notice it at the back of my mind, like background music.

Then, at other times, when I find myself confused, angry, or puzzled, I deliberately switch it on and it can be a channel of patience, hope or calmness.

### Notes

### Calling God 'You'

In my reviews of prayer, I have come to realise how much I called God 'You' during my prayer. I was saying, 'You were at work there!' 'You were behind that gift!' and 'You are showing me!' etc. I talked to God as I would to another person facing me. This is not sending prayers out into outer space, with a fear that they would be lost out there, as I had been doing previously. Nor is it just thinking about what God might do, etc. As I said before, 'thinking about' is not prayer, though it can be a good preparation for it. Now, I am realising that I have spontaneously turned to God, am calling God 'You' and am now beginning to really pray, i.e. talk to God heart to heart.

*Symbols and special experiences of God*

Sometimes, during a deep prayer, someone may see a *symbol* that summarises the whole experience of feeling God being close and helping. For example, if one is feeling lost, the image of a guiding hand may come to mind and give comfort or a part-icular *memory* of God's saving help in some frightening crisis.

In an early workshop on prayer that I attended, the speaker kept repeating, 'If you want to meet God, go back to where you met him before.' These words influenced me greatly. They are good words also for summing up this whole chapter!

# CHAPTER EIGHT

## Asking my own God for Help
### Prayer of Petition (Part 1)

I now wish to talk about the prayer of petition and to reflect on how valuable this form of prayer is for bringing us closer to God and to one another.

In the prayer of petition we come to God with what we want, what we desire, and we know from experience how much felt 'wants' can move us. They give us energy for effort. What I want, what I really desire, can move me more readily and energetically than what I have to do as a matter of duty. Asked why we do something, we will generally find at the centre of our reason: 'It is because I want ...'

On our part, the effectiveness of our prayer of petition rests on the awareness that 1) we are talking to our own God, and 2) the growing awareness of what it is we really want.

### I. AWARENESS OF TALKING TO 'MY OWN GOD'

What we have done till now should help develop this awareness. We have seen the value of the mantra. So, my first step in a prayer of petition is to use my mantra to bring me before my 'own God' – the God I am coming to experience.

I begin by using my mantra till I feel I am back into remembering God's kindness to me. Then I change to repeating my mantra with the request added on, to the God I have come to know and believe in. Then I wait.

*The mistake of 'talking to the want'*
Our experience will probably confirm that it is easier for us to be focused more on what we want than upon the One whom we are talking to about the want. We often do not notice how very vague we are about who it is we are asking to help us. I remem-

ber the speaker at one of the first prayer workshops I attended used to call this 'Talking to the want.' It is not talking to God. It is really talking to ourselves about the want, expecting God to listen in and then do as we have decided.

Even now, I can discover myself committing this fault, even after many years of telling others about this danger. This is because when we feel a want very intensely, it is inclined to take us over. We almost drown in it. So, that is why we have to deliberately begin by focusing on the One to whom we are talking.

*It may require a lot of time*

When we are 'drowning' in the want, it can take a lot of time till we feel we are back before our own God. Indeed, don't be surprised that, in times of intense feelings such as pain or fear or anger, it might take most of the prayer exercise time just to get back to meeting him. It might even take all the time. The waiting might need to be carried over to the next time we do the exercise. But no matter how long it takes, we first wait to become aware of our own God.

### II. GROWING AWARENESS OF WHAT I REALLY WANT

The second step is then telling God what I want. The more concretely, honestly and correctly we express our want, the better the prayer can become.

*Concrete and clear*

I find that being specific helps me to focus better. So rather than just asking God to give me patience, it is better to say, for example, 'God give me patience towards ...' or 'God give me patience in the Thursday morning meeting'. This can also mean that when I get that help, I can recognise it more quickly and be thankful to God for answering me.

*'Dressing up'*

At times we may feel that we must appear before God as we think we should be or as we would like to be. For example, we can tend to be afraid to show anger before God – especially if our anger is towards God. We may feel that it is an insult to God to show him our worst side. So we feel the inclination to 'dress up' before praying. But this is not being honest. It is not being present as 'we really are'. Such 'dressing up' is a barrier that keeps us at a distance from God.

### Changing ourselves

This inclination can lead us into another mistake. We feel the urge to change ourselves by our own efforts before we appear before God. Clearly this is the opposite of what we are discovering. We don't have the power to change ourselves. It is God who changes us. In fact, it is especially in our embarrassment and helplessness, shown honestly to God, that we can experience him bringing about change in us. Our contribution is to be present with honesty and openness and trust in his transforming power. We put ourselves before him 'as we are', just like we do before the barber, dentist or surgeon, to wait and allow ourselves to be changed.

### Saying 'God already knows'

We may say, 'God already knows what I want so I don't have to tell him'. My answer is 'Yes, God knows. But the problem is we may not.' And that hinders our talking to God about what we really want.

### Knowing oneself

Knowing what we really want requires growing in self-knowledge. We all have a tendency to fool ourselves about ourselves. So knowing ourselves better and better is part of our spiritual journey towards closeness to God and others. This will be discussed later in greater detail.

### These awarenesses needed for all prayers of petition

As in the prayer exercises, the two awarenesses of my own God and of my own wants are needed in the simple requests for ourselves or others that we make, spontaneously, to God throughout our day. The prayer-exercises also train us to do these spontaneous prayers.

### NOTICING HOW GOD MIGHT ANSWER OUR PETITIONS

*Getting what we asked*

The clearest reason for believing that God has heard us and answered us is when we receive what we asked, e.g. the sickness gone, the worry solved, a chance for a new start.

*Getting something better*

At times when we don't get what we asked exactly, we later suddenly realise we got something connected to it, but better. This usually takes longer to recognise.

*Coming closer to God*

We may still be asking for what we want and not getting it. Yet, we suddenly realise that through asking, we have come closer to God. This gift of closeness is his answer to our petition. This may take even more time to discover.

*Changes in oneself*

Changes in oneself can come as a surprise discovery but this takes time. We might continue asking for something and not get it, but we notice that we are becoming more thankful, or patient, or generous in our daily living. Then we begin to recognise that we have changed for the better. This is how God may answer us. For example, many years ago I used to pray a lot for trust, and God didn't answer as I expected. It was only after doing the Good Things Prayer for a few years that I realised that the exercise was changing me to trust more. I suddenly recognised that this was how God was answering me.

*Discovering when God answers us*
We may discover God's answers:
* during a prayer time.
* later, during reflection time.
* when we are sharing deeply with another.
* due to some special happening in our daily lives.
* after repeating the prayer for a long time.

*Try it and see*
This explanation of how to do the prayer of petition may seem complicated and unnecessary. But, just think, is it not like reading the directions for how to use a new washing machine or camera that we are taking out of the box for the first time? Reading the instructions seems a nuisance indeed, but it certainly helps. Yet, using the new machine soon becomes automatic and easy and we wonder why it seemed so daunting at the beginning.

# CHAPTER NINE

# Meeting God in a Painful Experience

So far we have concentrated on letting good things bring us closer to God. Now we will look at how painful experiences also can do this. Who has no experience of pain – physical, mental or emotional – and in many different levels of intensity? What we have learned so far by praying through good things should help prepare us better to receive a new closeness to God discovered through painful experiences. Normally it takes more endurance and time to realise this but, for me, it seems to be a more vivid and influential discovery.

Our normal reaction to our painful, sleepless nights or help-less days is to spontaneously and often cry out to God for relief and rescue. As the pain of family tragedy, failure of a project, a broken relationship, unjust treatment or such, impinges strongly on us, we find ourselves pleading to be helped. We may even find ourselves crying, 'Why me?' or 'Why did you allow this?'

I have found that, besides these spontaneous pleas, making prayer exercises on such pain has helped me to eventually notice God in the experience and become closer to him. This means de-ciding on a particular length of time to talk to God about the pain. I am sure the framework of the exercise conditions me to be able to hear God better. I will give an example from the time I was just beginning to discover the value of prayer exercises.

*A story*
I had been feeling hurt and angry for some time. There had been different occasions when I felt that someone whom I had put ef-fort and enthusiasm into helping had treated me unfairly. I prayed about it often but I was not able to let go of this hurt feel-ing or put it aside.

One day this person had done something that particularly

annoyed me and I felt churned up inside. So to get some inner peace, I decided to go and pray about it for one hour. I went into the chapel. I often walked up and down as I prayed there. I started walking and repeating, 'Lord, I forgive him' as I believed a good Christian and I, as a priest, should do. But all the things I had done for him, contrasting with how I felt I had been ignored, were bursting up into my prayer like bubbles when water is starting to boil. I kept suppressing these, going back to 'Lord, I forgive him'. At times I would feel strongly my yearning for inner peace but I kept repeating, 'Lord, I forgive him'. I kept this up for about half-an-hour. I can remember that, even though I was trying doggedly, the prayer was a heavy, lifeless kind of prayer.

*The change*

Suddenly, something happened within me. I seemed to waken up from something. I became alive with energy. I stopped in front of the altar. I realised I was terribly angry. I wanted so much to chastise him. I shook my head and loudly proclaimed, 'No, I will not forgive. After this prayer I am going to call him and blast him. I am angry with him and I am angry with you, God, for not stopping him doing this to people.'

I continued to walk up and down, now very energetically, expressing these feelings. As the hour of prayer moved on there were moments when I felt a little more peaceful but then new memories of hurts or slights would pop up again and off I would go again telling God, in much detail, how annoyed I felt about them.

God seemed to be listening and understanding, indeed, to be inviting me to tell him all. I had the feeling that God was there, walking up and down with me. He was not annoyed or angry but, rather, understanding. But then, almost imperceptibly my prayer seemed to change. God gently awakened me to a wider horizon of things. At the same time I felt he was strengthening me. Gradually I began to feel uneasy. An uncomfortable feeling that I was about to see something I was not going to like, began to stir in me.

Little questions began to surface. Had I not built up expect-ations that were unrealistic? Did I want to give help even more than this person wanted to receive help? Why? Was it because I wanted to be well thought of? Or to organise things as I thought they should be? Were my helping and my 'good deeds' not trig-gered by unconscious wants or needs of my own? Was that fair to this person? With a shock I realised that I had been unaware of such motivations in myself. The realisation hit me; it was I who needed to be forgiven by him. I came out from the chapel a more contrite and humble man.

## Reflection
Afterwards I did a lot of reflection on this experience. I am going to sum up under four headings some of the things I learned from it: about God himself, about myself, about prayer and about for-giveness.

## Pause
Before reading further, pause to ask yourself what lessons you can learn from this story.

### WHAT I LEARNED ABOUT GOD

In the reflection I noticed that surprise was the strongest and most frequent feeling I had during the last part of this experi-ence. Firstly, I was amazed at feeling that God was walking up and down with me. I felt 'This is unbelievable.' I expected that I should feel afraid. After all, not only had I shown a stubborn anger before God but I had shown it towards him. And yet, here was he, walking with me, supporting and encouraging. Instead of feeling afraid, this was giving me a feeling of closeness. I was amazed.

I also found sadness and embarrassment at myself which eventually turned into a deeper feeling of gratitude to God.

I was awed at how expertly and graciously God had been able to begin to open my eyes and to change me. He was able to turn me around 180 degrees – and I didn't resist! I could not imagine anyone else being able to tell me, or show me, such motivations in myself. Yet God could do it, and in such a gentle, gradual way that I could accept it without resistance.

I was also amazed at the extent of God's patience. During the prayer time he was so patient with me when I was angry – and mistaken in my anger at that. Then I realised that he had been watching me fooling myself all the years till then in this and other ways. He had seen, for example, how much of my hard work was often from an unconscious desire to feel important. He had waited for a time when I would be able to hear and accept these real truths about myself and that certainly took patience.

Gradually I realised that, although God wanted me to change and to accept his help to change, in the meantime, he still fully accepted me as I was.

Since childhood, one of the things I had been taught about God was his patience, and I believed it, and had myself spoken about it to others. However, through this prayer experience, I had learned it in a new way. Like my experience of electricity and learning by discovery which I referred to earlier, I now knew these things in my very bones.

*Pause*
In reflection on praying in your own painful experiences, have you discovered any closer knowledge of God?

### WHAT I LEARNED ABOUT MYSELF

I came out of the chapel shocked, humble and contrite as well as grateful. I didn't feel crushed by what God had shown me. I felt very sobered. I had learned some 'home truths' about myself. I was very conscious that God had to do much more work in me than I had recognised and I had to co-operate with him in a greater way to accomplish it. Indeed I had a long journey ahead of me, but at the same time, I felt I had come closer to God and felt greater trust.

God had shown me a strong feeling of anger in myself. Till

this time, I had considered myself as a 'mild' person. Finding in myself such strong feelings of anger and revenge had unsettled me. Discovering how I had fooled myself was another shock. I had always prided myself on being honest, but here were signs that I was not as honest with myself as I had imagined. And I had not been aware of some of my own needs that had influenced me so much.

I realise now that I was able to accept these sobering revelations about myself because of the strong feeling that God walked with the real me and accepted me as I am. This brought feelings of gratitude and trust which drew me closer to God and made me more understanding and compassionate to others.

*Pause*
Can you think of anything you learned about yourself from praying in painful experiences? How do you feel about it?

WHAT I LEARNED ABOUT PRAYER

### Start praying from the feelings
From the experience I got a very compelling lesson about not 'dressing up' before God. As I have said before, this means not praying from the 'me' I think I *should* be but from the 'me' I really am. It also showed me that my feelings are closer to the core of the real me. Earlier, I had even heard that, in prayer, feelings do not count. This taught me otherwise. So when, a little later, I went to a workshop on prayer and the guide kept saying, 'Get in touch with the feelings', I easily understood. I realised I should have started off the prayer saying, 'I can't forgive' or 'I won't forgive' and relied on God to do something about me and, as I discovered, change the real me before him and not an imaginary me that did not exist.

### Give God his turn
Another very important thing that I learned is that I must not run away after pouring out rebellious or mean feelings at God. There is the temptation to 'hit and run', afraid of what I might

hear in return. Instead, I must wait and give God his turn to be heard. This, of course, is not easy because to wait like this requires trust in God's goodness to me. It also requires belief that God is great enough to take all my anger and not be repulsed by it nor change his attitude to me. But it does require 'fastening my seat belt' to keep me anchored before him.

*Value of prayer exercises*
Of course, I recognise that God's help can show itself at any time and in any way and can not be programmed by us. But this experience was strong confirmation of the value of prayer exercises which I was beginning to learn about at this time. As you saw, in this tough experience I had decided to pray for an hour and so stayed during the lifeless, tedious prayer. Then, after I erupted, I still had to stay. And it was in the remainder of the hour that God was able to get through to me.

My experience also taught me that it takes some time after pouring out negative feelings at God, before I can begin to notice God moving my heart to positive feelings of being precious to him. So let us remember to wait, wait, wait.

This is a good, concrete example of an experience in which I was convinced I was meeting God. I could use it before other prayer times to go back to the conviction of his presence.

Of course, this prayer experience did not solve my emotional problem all at once. I found I had to go back to God many more times to talk about this feeling, but I was able to do it better.

I began to realise that praying in a deep condition of pain from loss, fear, yearning, anger or worry is a special place for eventually meeting God at a new level.

And as usual the experience from the prayer exercise greatly influenced my spontaneous prayer.

### WHAT I LEARNED ABOUT FORGIVENESS

This incident taught me not to presume my strength to forgive but to recognise my limits and to start praying from there. It also led me to a deeper understanding of the connection between receiving forgiveness and granting it and coming to appreciate the 'Forgiving God'. I will say more about this later, in Chapter 12.

### In other pains

I gave an example from an emotional pain of resentment. But prayer exercises like this can also be used in the pain from fear, worry, grief or sickness, etc.

### Questions

Have you noticed any changes in your prayer?

Have you noticed any changes in yourself because of your times in prayer?

Any other discoveries?

# CHAPTER TEN

## *Showing God what I really want*
### *Prayer of Petition (Part 2)*

*Recap*

In this book, I delayed talking about the prayer of petition until we established a foundation for it. I pointed out how easy it is to make the mistake of concentrating more on the request than on the One to whom we are making the request. The prayer exercises we had been doing before Chapter 8 should have helped in building up the habit of first turning to God very consciously.

Also highlighted was the difference between making a request 'out of the head' and making it from deeper within oneself. I often pointed out how being aware of our feelings brings us into this inner world in ourselves. Noticing our feelings helps us to recognise parts of ourselves that, previously, we had not paid attention to or had been unaware of. This self knowledge can, in turn, lead us into a deeper closeness to God. It is open-ended; it can get deeper and deeper.

In this getting to know our real inner self better, we must have noticed how much prayer exercises contributed to this. They gave us space, time, focus and receptivity for accepting these revelations about self.

*Going deeper*

In this chapter, I want to deal with going deeper into self knowledge by using prayer exercises of petition. I will start off by giving a concrete example. As usual, I rely on repetition of words to help me stay focused, to wait, and to share with God.

So, for example, I want to get this book finally finished. In a planned prayer exercise I turn to God and ask for help. While repeating my mantra and request, I gradually become aware that I am praying out of a feeling of frustration. Showing this to God, I begin to feel uneasy that maybe God might not want the book finished. I feel resistance to accepting that possibility. I have put so much work into it so far. Some people have said it could be a useful book. I could not 'let go' with docility. I show this honestly to God. My head says, 'If God wants a book like this, he can provide it without me. Let go in trust.' But I can find no willingness in myself to accept this. Showing this resistance to God, I realise I have a very limited amount of trust. And then I start a new petition, 'Lord, I want more trust.'

Or the idea that maybe God just wants it postponed and more work done on it, presents itself. I find resistance to accepting even this. Telling God this begins to make me aware that I want the satisfaction of completing and achieving something. This leads further to noticing that I want to impress, be appreciated and well thought of. I show these to God and wait.

Or, the resistance to putting aside the book leads me to recognising that I want this tidied up now and then get on to the next project. I gradually acknowledge how restless I am inside. I am continually being pulled along by the lure of 'what next?' It can lead me to end up praying for patience.

*What happens (The process)*
In this way, a fairly lengthy petition prayer-exercise can lead us into deeper self knowledge. I imagine it like a miner being brought down the mineshaft in a cage that lets him see the different layers in the earth. I see the deeper wants underneath the one I started with.

I am not advocating self-analysis here. I emphasise that God shows me as I wait with openness. So, simply stated, the process, shorn of its distractions and wanderings, goes something like this. In a prayer exercise of repeating a request to my own God, I become more aware of how I feel at that time. I continue by sharing this feeling with God. I become aware of a new want coming into my consciousness. I accept this, sometimes with reluctance, and now spend my time sharing this with God and waiting for him to work on me. I finish up praying from a deeper or more basic want.

*Results*

Thinking about the example, it is understandable how we can be led to recognising in ourselves feelings such as anxiety, insecurity, loneliness, fear, resentment, jealousy, weariness. This can make us aware of a want to be in control, feel superior, seeking stimulation, always to feel beyond criticism, overcautious to put insights into practice and so on. This eventually can lead to bringing a new, deeper want to God.

*Review*

Reflecting on the process, I realise that I have experienced God revealing to me more of myself. At the same time, he is accepting this 'me'. This helps me to accept that same self. I also realise that God, through his working in me, is revealing more of himself to me. In any relationship, the more 'real' and open and accepting of each other we are, the deeper the relationship becomes. It is the same with our relationship to God. So, a reciprocal thing happens: the closer we come to God, the more of our real selves is revealed to us and the more our real self is revealed, the closer we can come to God. It is a deepening spiral.

So, even if we do not get what we specifically request, a growing closeness to God may be the answer. Actually, I think I have been brought closer to God more by his seeming to ignore my request than by having it granted. In review, I ask myself could this closeness be what God wants. And deep down, I begin to discover that is what I want too. So, really, the deeper we go, the more we realise that our own basic wants and God's wants are the same. And as I said before, we can do things more readily because we want to, rather than because we are told we 'must do'. We have more energy for them.

*Liberated*

By showing these newly discovered compelling wants to God, we can become less their slave. We discover that, not only are they stronger and more basic, but they have been influencing our behaviour in unrecognised ways till now. Like in the story in Chapter 9 and my struggles with forgiveness, we are brought out of a more idealistic idea of ourselves into a more real one. We find that what supports our attitudes and drives our actions is a mixture of our ideal motives and these deeper, unnoticed wants. Unfortunately the latter exert the more control on us. Coming to recognise them, accepting them, and asking God to work on them, frees us to see and choose to act better for the benefit of ourselves or others. Though, of course, it still requires much generosity and effort on our part.

So, we need not be surprised to find resistance to accepting these revelations. For example, we may notice a fear that, if these things are true, no one could like us and we would finish up isolated from everyone, and so we are tempted to postpone accepting these budding revelations. Or the suspicion that to face up to them and to allow the changes to happen at this time, will demand too much generosity, self-discipline and perseverance on our part. It is only the experiences of God accepting us 'as we are' that strengthen us sufficiently to accept ourselves more and more and journey deeper into this close relationship. This is also a growth in maturity. It makes us more honest with others, more understanding of others, and so we come closer to them as well as to God.

Later, we come to recognise that we have been using a lot of energy, throughout our lives, to hide these truths from ourselves.

Freed from this resistance, we can now use this energy to do other good things. Resistance to knowing and accepting ourselves can cause stress, which can affect our health, while self-acceptance can bring inner peace and healing.

But, I think, the greatest fruit is greater recognition of not only God working *in* us and in our weaknesses, but working *through* us. We find ourselves, more and more, in gratitude, passing on God's gifts to others.

*The strength of gratitude*
If you come to prayer feeling grateful, stay with that feeling. As you remain gratefully present to God, you may become aware of new invitations. These show us deeper wants within us. So wait until God shows these to you. The feeling of thanks will strengthen you to accept what is shown. So cherish this feeling of gratitude for as long and as fully as you can.

It is my experience that God helps us to know our true selves only in as much as we are strong enough to accept what he shows us. God waits until we are ready.

*Longer prayer exercises?*
One result of this chapter may be examining oneself about the length of the prayer exercises. Am I giving enough time?

# CHAPTER ELEVEN

## The 'But start with me' Prayer
### Praying for Another Person to Change

I have been in situations where working, living or dealing with another person has made me wish for God to move us apart or change the other. And I have prayed hard for this. But, normally, the prayer would soon fall into thinking about the faults of the other and my negative feelings would take over. I would end up in turmoil, no better than I started. The discovery I am going to talk about now has helped harness the energy from these strong feelings, leading to fruitful change in myself, greater closeness to God and to others.

*Discovering the 'start with me' prayer*
When I was beginning my serious study into prayer, I listened to tapes by a laywoman. One of her topics concerned praying for someone else to be changed in some way. She gave, as an example, the religious conversion of her husband. She told how, for many years, she had been praying for his conversion but it didn't happen. Then she felt moved to change her prayer to 'Lord, change my husband, but start with me.' Some time afterwards, to her amazement, he told her that he had joined a class preparing for baptism. So, in her talk she recommended that always, when we pray for another to change, we lengthen the prayer to, 'Lord, change ... but start with me!' and emphasise the latter part.

I used it, at first, for a situation of strong feelings of frustration and dislike, but I find it may be used for any situation where there is a desire that another person be changed in some way. This can be someone we like or someone we don't like, a friend or an antagonist, a close member of the family or it could be a group, a fellow worker or one's boss, a superior or a dependant and so on. The thing to keep in mind is, after asking for change in another, to add and emphasise, 'but start with me!' Maybe there will be no change in the other but there will be in me and this praying for another has begun it.

### THE EXERCISE – AND THE 'TRIANGLE'

So I made it into an exercise for myself which I call the 'triangle'. As with other exercises, we begin by deciding for how long, we turn to our own God and ask him to change the person or situation but to start with me.

#### The first point of the triangle: 'My own God' at work

The first point of the triangle is bringing ourselves before our own God. The truth that God desires and is working to save all may come into our mind strongly. We might find ourselves repeating 'You are at work to save.' As we continue, a wider view of things opens up. We become more aware that God is looking at the whole situation, including this person or situation. But the reasons why we want the person changed can intrude and take over our attention and energy. This moves us to the second point of the triangle.

#### Second point: God's relationship to the one we want changed

Now we repeat something like, 'You are working to save; please, change …' The other person is filling our minds now; the black spots keep popping up. We feel our reactions to them. We feel strongly we want this person changed. For a while we may be held there. However, it can begin to penetrate our consciousness that God also must see the faults in this person and his saving desire wants this person's growth even more than we do. Yet, it looks like God can wait for this person to change. Because we do not like waiting, this causes an uneasy feeling in us and brings us to the third point of the triangle.

#### Point three: our own relationship with God

We still feel it is right to ask God to change the other and we keep asking. Awareness of our own attitudes may come into play here and we notice a tendency to focus on the other's faults when, in fact, another question is nudging in: 'Am I concerned for the change in this person for his or her own good or is it primarily for how it affects me?' In other words, how much does this desire to change the other come out of our own self interest? This challenges us to wait and see.

We may be brought back to God's saving action, to his desire to save this person, and his patience and generosity. We begin to feel challenged to see our need and to accept God's gift of more patience, understanding or generosity towards this person. Here we may feel resistance and resentment because if this person did not need to change, then we would not have to subject ourselves to all this struggle. 'But start with me' helps us to stay in this feeling till something changes in us.

### The triangle at work

Each prayer exercise develops differently. For example, the third point may become simply, 'Lord, make me more ...' Or 'change ...' may intrude again leading to contemplating God desiring to save everyone and then, perhaps, awakening us to a need for personal change of which we were unaware. And so it goes.

### A long-range prayer

It seems to me that the stronger my emotional desire for change in another is, the more often I have to do this prayer. But I also find that the same strong emotions fuel my concentration and my stamina. I have only to turn to the urge to change the other to refocus myself and feel new energy.

### Fruit

At a personal level, each of us may notice even small changes in ourselves. For example, during the day we discover, to our surprise, that we have acted with unusual patience or generosity or tolerance towards the person we have been praying for. Or we may find that we are less critical and more tolerant towards people in general. And so we return thanks.

I find too in the course of a day that, while feeling annoyed with or thinking critically of someone, I suddenly seem to wake up and begin asking, 'Lord, start with me.' I realise how these exercises have schooled me for this spontaneous prayer and in the need and openness to change.

Flowing from this prayer is that I notice a growing habit of making an effort to compliment people when I recognise even small but admirable things in them. I do not mean flattery, which is dishonest and manipulating, but genuine acknowledgement.

*Reflection*

Since this exercise helps to lead to greater self-knowledge, helps change us, gives a closer union with God and a gradually changing attitude to other people, I suspect that God uses the struggles of daily life to bring about changes in us that make us more like himself.

I am becoming more aware that everyone needs to keep changing till they die. God is continually calling each of us to grow into being a 'special' person with his help. This growth is greatly influenced by our relations with others – both by the good relationships and the difficult ones. We are always learning that we can only change ourselves. But as we do change we often make it easier for others around us to change too. So I find this prayer exercise a valuable one indeed. It is one important aspect of meeting God in relationships.

## CHAPTER TWELVE

# *Prayer and Forgiveness*

### I. THE CHALLENGE OF FORGIVENESS

In a book on prayer, it is impossible to avoid the question of forgiveness. As we journey deeper into prayer and closeness to God, he keeps leading us into this challenging world of forgiveness. It certainly is a place we naturally don't want to enter.

*Our experiences of injury and injustice*
Without doubt we all have, in different ways, experienced being hurt, unjustly treated, neglected, betrayed or such. We have felt deeply the anger, sadness or fear that it could happen again. We have strongly reacted by complaining, wanting to punish, to overcome, or at least to change the culprit. As you read this, you may even be experiencing something like this at the present moment. At least, we have had experiences like these in the past. Even if we think we have forgotten them we will discover that, if we give them a chance to come back to memory, they will do so and, to our surprise, strongly and with the same old fierce feelings and reactions.

*The instinct to protect oneself*
We recognise that there is a natural human instinct to protect ourselves from hurt and injury. The idea of forgiving seems like we are not protecting ourselves. To forgive would seem to be deliberately welcoming the loss of something important to us. Therefore, the opposite, namely 'not to forgive' would seem to be a good thing. And if it is a good thing, it must come from God. Thus, not forgiving should increase our inner thanks and peace. But does our experience confirm this? No! Our experience shows us that the condition of 'not forgiving' causes unrest, dissatisfaction, bitterness and coldness in our hearts. So, 'not to forgive' can not be what God wants.

*So where is God leading us? – and why?*
Indeed our prayer experience seems to show that God wants us to forgive those who injure us. The deeper our prayer becomes, the more we become aware of the challenge to forgive. In our daily living, we seem to become more sensitive to new hurts and injuries. Painful memories of the past which we thought were well buried and forgotten are now, surprisingly, coming back into our prayer and into our daily consciousness. People who hurt us in the past and whom we thought we were finally free of, come back into our lives and we are again in the struggle to forgive. We realise more and more that forgiveness plays a big part in our spiritual life.

*Christians and forgiveness*
Of course, as Christians we know that forgiveness is central to Christ's teaching, and was a central part of his own actions towards others. It is tied in very closely to his resurrection and thus to new life in us.

*Explaining forgiveness from the experience of a 'praying human'*
However, in this book I want to talk only from my experience of 'praying as a human'. So I have come to answer my question using the following analogy. I used to imagine forgiveness as something like papering over an ugly hole made in a wall. Nobody can now see the hole though it is still there. I used to think forgiveness was like that. Now I compare forgiveness to freely rebuilding a whole new wall, and doing so as often as the wall is damaged.

Likewise, I used to think forgiveness meant deliberately trying to return to the relationship that existed before the injury and forcing myself to imagine that it hadn't happened. Now I understand it as recognising, fully, that it did happen but, in spite of that injury, I now want to make a whole new relationship with the person who injured me. It is a new attitude, energy or life that is beginning to grow in me. True forgiveness will include a desire that the other be blessed and happy, even if it is of no benefit to me. Thus, it has no self-interest but is centred on benefit to the other person. Forgiving is giving birth; it is offering a new life to someone. It is a purely generous gift. I want to be an instrument of good for the other. This forgiveness will result in an even deeper relationship than before the injury. This is a central point.

### Being able to forgive is a gift from God
My own experience and understanding of being able to forgive someone has led me ultimately to realise that to forgive another shows that God has given me a special gift. I have become more like God and am acting more like God. Therefore, to forgive is not a loss but a gain. Indeed, the one forgiving receives the greater gift.

### We must first experience being forgiven
Of course, as we shall see, before we can forgive we have to experience the gift of being forgiven! Thus, when we can forgive, we really have received two gifts: being forgiven and being able to forgive. Through both experiences we deepen our relationship with God and with other people. At the same time, we must recognise how difficult it is to receive these gifts.

#### II. STEPS IN PRAYING TO BE ABLE TO FORGIVE

Really, what is harder to do than truly forgive? Obviously, it does need special strength from much prayer. In my praying about forgiveness, I go through the following steps:

### Praying 'I can't forgive'
I find myself in a condition where I don't want to do much else but pray for liberation from my hurt feelings. Because I feel like I am trapped in an emotional blizzard, my times for prayer increase. Firstly, spontaneously, many times during the day and night, I cry out to be freed from this turmoil.

Secondly, I make special times, i.e. prayer exercises, to pray about this problem. Before each time, I decide how long I am going to pray about it. Then I turn to God and ask him to lead me out of this terrible turmoil.

As I begin the prayer I recognise I expect God to help me. I repeat things like 'God, I am hurting', 'help me', 'I am angry', 'free me'. I know I was told that God wants me to forgive. But at this time my hurt feelings and convictions are just too strong to be able to do so. I simply can not. So I have to start my prayer for forgiveness from the honest condition of recognising and repeating, 'I can't forgive. I can't forgive.'

Maybe nothing changes much and that is how I end the prayer time. So, at the next prayer time, I begin where I left off, by repeating 'I cannot forgive.' And if necessary, at the next time and the next time, and I keep doing this till something new does happen!

### 'I won't forgive'

Sometimes I even unearth a feeling of 'Even if I could forgive, I will not.' I just have to hold this stubborn, obstinate feeling before God and wait for some new movement within myself.

### Seeing times I needed forgiveness

The first change I usually experience is something like the following. Into my head gradually come memories of times when I was stupid, selfish, neglectful or hurt others and needed forgiveness.

### Realising God forgives me

Then I begin to realise that I wasn't punished or even shamed because of these. In fact, at times such as these God seemed to give me special gifts that were helpful for myself and others. I did nothing to earn these. God gave them to me freely. I begin to realise God is showing me times when he forgave me.

### Accepting forgiveness isn't easy

I am also learning that not only offering forgiveness but accepting it is not easy. Because it means I must first be conscious that I have done wrong, I try to avoid accepting that fully. Even if I do recognise it, I am inclined to put it out of my mind. Or I may concentrate on trying to first correct my fault by my own efforts, in order that I can imagine I didn't really do much wrong. All these natural reactions are working inside me to avoid accepting that I needed forgiveness and got forgiveness, without earning it in any way.

### God has already forgiven us even before we ask

When I am told that God has already forgiven me since the moment I first did the wrong – before I even asked for forgiveness – it is even harder to believe. It makes me ask myself, 'Then why ask for forgiveness?' I answer myself by saying, 'It is part of my recognising that I need it, as well as recognising God's generous goodness.' Spending time on the need opens my heart to accept it with gratitude and trust. It reminds me of the sun shining outside my room window but, until I open the curtains, the light can not pour in. In the same way, I have to open my penitent heart to accept the forgiveness which God has already granted.

### Being led towards forgiving others

Often, the next change in my prayer is the appearance of possible reasons why the other person might have become such a person to act like that towards me. I don't go searching for these but I notice them beginning to appear. These cause my attitude towards the other to become less severe. I have had experiences of suddenly being given a chance to do something good for that person and being able to do it easily and without thinking, causing me to be greatly surprised at myself.

Even when I cannot forgive, I find I can, to some extent, pray for the other to be blessed. And this can lead into the 'start with me' prayer of Chapter 11.

### Growth in accepting and granting forgiveness

But all these are signs that I am growing in being able to accept forgiveness as well as becoming able to forgive. Actually, accepting forgiveness and granting forgiveness are bound together. Growth in one means growth in the other.

### III. DISCOVERIES

During our forgiveness prayer we may discover strong reasons why someone must be corrected or punished, smothering any movement towards forgiveness. It causes struggle in us until a small voice seems to say, 'Yes, this person should be corrected. But are you the one to do it? With what heart do you want to correct him?' And we realise we want to do it from an angry, punishing, self-righteous, aggressive heart. Then we realise that it is more important to have our own heart changed first.

I remember once, after I had prayed myself into peace and forgiveness towards an offending person, I suddenly imagined an approaching occasion when I might be hurt again. Back flooded the turmoil and anger and I had to pray till the inspiration jumped into my mind, 'It's simple, if you are hurt again, why not just forgive again? After all, *that is what God does.*' And suddenly, this took away all my turmoil and, surprisingly, gave me a happy, positive outlook instead.

*Having to go through the process again – and again – and again*
I have had the experience of finally praying myself into peace and forgiveness, and feeling I was a whole different person. Then I have found in my daily living I had lost this good attitude, and have had to climb the steps again – from the bottom. We often go through the process again and again, but each time we gain new strength.

*Specialising in Forgiveness*
We will always find coming into our consciousness new people who have to be forgiven. God wants us to experience his forgiving love and new life flowing into us and through us to others. I am also convinced that each one has a special power to help the person who hurt him or her greatly – the greater the hurt the greater the potential to help. We will find too, that we are led

back into our oldest and strongest relationships to forgive things, e.g. conflicts with family, tensions with oldest friends. These seem to be the hardest to do and the last ones we can face. Yet, we are often led back into them. God seems to want to really school us in forgiveness. He seems to want us to specialise in it. But this is consistent with discovering that God brings us closer to himself by making us one and more like himself, the forgiving God.

CHAPTER THIRTEEN

# *Sharing about Our Spiritual Journeys*
### *Help for one another*

My own experience, and the experience of many who have participated in these prayer exercises, is that sharing with others about their discoveries in prayer has increased manifoldly the good effects of the prayer. In this chapter I want to talk about sharing. I am thinking of two people sharing or a small group sharing. A large group can be divided into different smaller groups.

It can be so fruitful. In fact all I have written in this book has come out of stacks of notes on my reflections after praying and sharing about these with others. But first, I want to state clearly what, in this book, I mean when I use the word 'sharing'.

## I. WHAT THE WORD 'SHARING' MEANS

The word 'sharing' can mean different things, at different times, to different people. For example, it can mean telling one's troubles to another to get sympathy or support or advice. This can be a very useful kind of sharing. But that is *not* what I am talking about in this book. Here is what I mean:

### The content of our sharing
When I say 'sharing' here, I mean to emphasise its two bases: noticing God's activity, and our own reflection on it. This sharing is about how each discovers God, what he is doing in their daily lives, and in their prayer times. It is also about their responses to this experience and about any effects or changes coming from it. Obviously, reflection is a necessary preparation for this kind of sharing.

*Sharing becomes easier and deeper*
I do not say sharing about inner experiences is easy. Even to notice them requires time and effort. Then to talk about them requires further effort. But it is encouraging to know that it becomes easier and more fruitful with practice. I will talk about different stages of it below. However, the following important points must be kept in mind.

*Must be done freely, respecting one's own privacy*
It is vitally important always to remember that sharing must be done freely. No one should feel that they 'have to share'. It means waiting for an inner inclination to share, even though it will probably require effort to do so.

It also means deciding about how much to share at any time. We must always respect our own privacy. We should feel free to choose what parts we want to share at any time. Whom we are with, our present mood, etc, will determine our decisions.

It is only when we are sure that we want to share this particular thing, here and now, that we should do so. If there is any doubt, wait. If we can't arrange our thoughts about what we experienced or how to say it, we are not ready to share. So we must wait.

*Good listening*
For fruitful sharing, listening is as valuable as speaking. One reason is that attentive listening helps another to share. It gives support and an unspoken message about the importance of the sharer. It is easy for a listener to fall into the mistake of 'half-listening' and, while someone else is sharing, to be mentally preparing their own material for sharing. This spoils good listening to another. One must listen and concentrate on what the other is sharing and trust God to help, if necessary, when the time comes for one's own sharing. Otherwise, it is enough to say 'I am not ready to share today; I will just listen to you others.' Without embarrassment, simply saying I have nothing to share today is itself good sharing.

If during a sharing period there is no one ready to share and everyone becomes silent, that is not a loss. It can be a very fruitful period of silence together.

Remember, we are told that the way we listen to another person tells us how we listen to God.

## Confidentiality
Of course, we must respect the privacy of others too, and be very careful to keep what is shared within the group.

## Why sharing is so fruitful
* *It deepens the sharer's own experience and insights*
  The effort needed to understand better my own experience, in order to tell another about it, makes the experience more vivid and deeper for myself.
* *Learning from what others share*
  Hearing others share of their discoveries of God working in their lives can help me to notice similar things that God is doing for me too, but which I hadn't noticed before this.
* *Wider awareness of God's action*
  Hearing how God is working in others too, and in so many different ways, gives me a much wider view and deeper admiration of God at work.
* *Consolation and closeness*
  If I share about a struggle, failure or slump while experiencing others not being critical or shocked, I am strengthened and consoled. If another shares about a failure to respond to God's gifts or invitations, it consoles me. I am relieved to know that I am not the only one who has failures or embarrassing weaknesses inside me.

  In fact this kind of sharing brings us closer together. We realise that we are weak, struggling people, journeying together, but trying to do our best. This sharing helps us to accept one another with understanding and compassion.

## Growth in sharing

Early, as we begin to learn the practice of sharing on prayer experiences, let us confine ourselves to searching for, and sharing good things only. Even if it seems only a very small good thing, start with that. In our prayer times there will be times of confusion, struggle or barrenness and to share the experiences can be very helpful. However, I don't recommend doing this until one has first had some experience of fruitful sharing about good things.

We will notice that we gradually begin to share more about how we feel as we discover these workings of God, e.g. joy, surprise, or gratitude. We will also be able to share about how we respond to these with trust, generosity, courage, or hope. Later, we will be able to talk about negative feelings too.

Remember this: we don't share about our troubles. But we do share about *how we talk with God* about our troubles.

Growth in sharing is part of our journey into intimacy with God, with self and with others. It is wrong to compare oneself to others. Each one's rate of growth is unique. It is important to develop at one's own pace. Even as we progress it is not at a steady pace. I think we move more like frogs – a series of staying put then taking a long leap foward!

## Silent prayer to begin

It can be very helpful before sharing for the sharers to be silent together for a few moments, aware of one another.

## Review of the sharing

It is also very fruitful to end the sharing by reviewing it silently for a few minutes. Each one could ask oneself questions such as, 'Did I get anything from this sharing?' 'Did I listen well?' 'Did everyone get a chance to share?'

## Examples of ways, places, times, etc for sharing

I encourage friends to make 'dates' for sharing. Even if a group is using this book to study prayer together and are sharing when they assemble, I still encourage other times or ways of sharing. If the group is only meeting once a month, this added time of sharing can be valuable. The ways of sharing may vary. It may be face-to-face in places such as a coffee shop, going for a walk together, a scheduled phone call. Agreeing on a set time and for how long helps this practice. It also can be done by e-mail, letter, tape, etc.

## II. FURTHER BENEFITS FROM SPIRITUAL SHARING

### Habit of praying with others

I have discovered that my own developing habit of sharing has helped me develop a better habit of praying with others. Now as I talk with someone about good news or bad news, I am more ready to say, 'Let's say a prayer of thanks together' or 'Let's ask together for guidance in this situation.' I find it is happening more spontaneously and frequently. When someone asks me to pray for something I usually say, 'Let's do it here and now.' Also, I might ask people who happen to be nearby to join us, because I believe that adds strength to the prayer.

### Family prayer

I think spiritual sharing can help to build a habit of family prayer. For example, before a meal together, pausing briefly to look at the good things in one's day, then making a few short prayers with these in mind, could help a family to pray more comfortably together.

### Building up a spiritual community

This type of sharing also helps build a good, spiritual community that prays together. The common focus is centred on what God is doing for, in, and through each one, leading to seeing what God is doing for, in, and through the group.

It gives greater mutual respect and a common spirit of gratitude. We realise that, while discussions can be divisive, sharing is very unifying – even where there are generation gaps, social gaps, cultural gaps, etc.

One of the most important things I have learned in my life and work as a priest is that developing the habit of listening and sharing can foster spiritual growth, unity and mutual support within a community!

### III. SPECIAL HELPERS FOR THE SPIRITUAL LIFE

It is important to be aware of the availability of help for spiritual growth that special, experienced 'spiritual helpers' or 'spiritual companions' can provide. There has always been in the church a tradition of such people. At some periods they have been more present than at others and their ways of helping have changed from time to time. At present there is a growing need for many such helpers. Thankfully, their numbers are gradually increasing, especially among lay people. Also, the way of spiritual help is becoming more like what it was in an earlier church.

Today in this ministry, the emphasis is on helping anyone who wants to grow spiritually. Even when things are going well, these seekers or 'travellers' still want both help to discover where they seem to be invited further, and support to move in that direction. So, the travellers visit the helpers on a regular schedule. They first talk about the good things that are happening before exploring together what new invitations to growth may be contained in their daily living and prayer. The helper, as a listener and a mirror, with patience, understanding and good questions, helps the traveller to recognise these invitations more clearly, and the decisions to be made. Responsibility for decisions must rest with the seeker.

At first, it might seem almost impossible, especially for lay people to find many such people. When I was young, these guides were all priests. Today many religious sisters and many lay people are proving themselves to be excellent spiritual helpers, and the numbers are increasing. Of course, the need for them is also increasing as, more and more, people become aware of the help for spiritual growth these people can give. I have received much help from many of them.

*Qualifications*

The necessary qualifications for a good helper are:

* To have, themselves, a good, steady prayer life.
* To have gained considerable experience from striving to develop their own spiritual life in the midst of good and bad conditions.
* To have considerable experience of being helped by spiritual companions.
* To have the ability to listen well, put people at ease, help them talk about their inner life, and about choices to be made.
* To have good common sense and good balance in making judgements.
* To have the ability to recognise and suggest when a more experienced person might be more helpful.
* To be themselves availing of supervision in their ministry.
* To have a desire to learn more about the spiritual life by study, attending guidance courses, reading, listening to talks, etc.

I dream of the day such helpers will be present and recognised in every community.

#### IV. A SPECIAL, WELL-DEVELOPED METHOD OF SHARING

Here is one example of a concrete, well-developed method of sharing. I have used it myself for three years with three other people – a sister and two lay women. As a group we decided to do it like this. Others may not want to, or be able to, do it in the same way, but may get hints from it. It is a form of 'group spiritual companioning.'

*Venue.* We meet once a month, for two hours, at an agreed time and place. One of the four agrees to be time-keeper.

*Start.* We start with 5 minutes silent prayer for guidance during the sharing.

*First Sharer.* For about 7-8 minutes, one of the four shares on the past month's prayer experiences – good things, struggles, wants, hopes, etc.

Then there is 3 minutes silence for pondering on that sharing and for the listeners to notice any effects it may have had on them.

Then one, two or three of the others, for no more than 2 minutes each, may share on how they were affected. This is not discussion or advice. But it is a form of feedback and may help the first sharer see new things in her/his experience.

Then there is another 3 minutes silence, mainly to pray privately for the person who has just shared.

*Second Sharer.* Another person shares for about 7-8 minutes – and the same procedure of silence and feedback follows.

*The Third and Fourth sharers* do likewise.

*Finish.* Then we usually finish up with about 4 minutes silent reflection of what each one got from the whole session.

*Next venue.* Finally, the place, time, etc of the next meeting is decided.

*If I can't attend.* Anyone who can not attend may, by letter, phone or by briefing another of the group, report on things he or she would like to share. After the report, the group prays for the absent person for 3 minutes but does not share on how the report affected them.

*Timekeeper.* We usually take turns at timekeeping and conducting the session.

*Hints.* As I said, not many might want to try something like this in the early stages of discovering deeper prayer, but it will give hints for the future. Also they may get tips or suggestions from it for improving their present ways of sharing, e.g. having more silent pauses.

*In the church of the future.* My hope is that in the church of the future, sharing times somewhat like this will become more and more common. Today, I notice examples of different sharing groups emerging in different communities.

# CHAPTER FOURTEEN

## For Groups

*Who is this book for?*
As I said before, the contents of this book were talks originally prepared for groups and influenced by the sharing of many groups. The first aim of this book was to help group leaders. The second aim was to provide a supplementary aid for individuals in such groups. Experience showed that individuals benefit from group prayer exercises. So from the start these talks had groups very much in mind.

But in publishing the book here, I had to recognise that there was more likelihood of an individual picking it up in a bookshop and trying out the exercises alone, experimenting with them and reflecting on them. This would make it into an individual's long-term, 'do-it-yourself' instruction manual.

So I chose to focus on the individual but with the intention of adding these two chapters on sharing and groups while suggesting throughout the book that the individual think about some kind of group participation. When I say 'group' I mean a number of people who meet regularly together to pray in silence for a definite period and then to review and to share on it. I consider anything from two people upwards to be a group. Thus, I hope the benefit of a group's help is realised.

*New groups*
Since I believe some participants will eventually feel drawn to co-operate in starting or leading new groups, for the remainder of this chapter I want to offer encouragement and some practical hints which experience taught me were helpful. I saw the value of three or four people leading a group. The team effort enhanced preparing for, and conducting, the prayer sessions. It lessened the burden on any one volunteer leader, especially one coping with unexpected events or obligations.

*Helpful points for leaders*
I offer the following suggestions:

Before a group begins, each participant meets with a leader who explains the aim of the programme, namely to help people to discover ways of coming closer to God and to others, especially through praying.

It is also important to talk about attendance and practice of the exercises between meetings.

A little about silence, listening and sharing is also practical here.

The duration of the course and the importance of commitment to faithful attendance is discussed.

*Group size*
Group size can vary greatly. Though I have had a few groups of over fifty people, my average was about twenty-five. Some participants have started new groups with just eight. In all these groups, for sharing, people divide into smaller groups of about three or four each. The big or small size of a group should not hinder its starting.

*Elements of a meeting*
For me, the essential elements of a meeting are: a short, guided, private review of what happened since the last meeting; an explanation about some aspect of prayer; some silent prayer time together; review and sharing about this; suggestions about practices till the next meeting.

*Frequency of meeting*
I started off by meeting weekly. Then I switched to twice a month and found it more practical and fruitful. Some groups chose to meet only monthly and received much help from this. But my own preference would be for twice a month. If less frequent, I would suggest that in twos or threes, participants should make private arrangements to share one more time between meetings, over coffee or by telephone or even email.

But the most important thing is how each individual prays and reviews in his/her own time between meetings.

*Further benefits from joining a group*
There are many advantages in following these talks as a group. The decision to join a group, and the effort to attend, prevents one from postponing or forgetting stages of the programme.

There is encouragement and stimulus from meeting the others.

There is the strength which praying with others gives.

There are the values of sharing which we have already seen in Chapter 13.

*Where*
My experiences come from groups in the church hall, in convent halls or in private homes. Private homes are being used more frequently, especially with some former participants uniting to become leaders of new groups.

*Attendance*
This book, more than just explaining about prayer, aims at stimulating practices. The talks are like steps of stairs, one talk built on the previous one. Thus, in a group, attendance from the beginning is essential. Also, regular attendance is very important. A meeting missed is to be supplemented before the next meeting by tapes, printouts or the guidance of another participant. A missed meeting, not supplemented, causes loss, not only to the person who was absent, but to the whole group's smooth progress. A commitment to regular attendance is necessary.

*Length of course*
For that reason, before starting, I would announce when the course would end and any special breaks or holidays. This helped some people to arrange their schedules and make a firm commitment to attend. After a course ended, participants who wanted more, would join a new group and repeat this course. It

was from these repeating participants that leaders of new groups eventually emerged.

*Sample meeting*
* *Opening Prayer* by leader or a member asked beforehand.
* *5/6 minutes guided review*. I usually ask about 5 questions with a pause in between. These questions are to help the participants notice any significant actions by God in their daily lives, especially since the last meeting or since the group began.
* *Talk* (about 20 mins) on a new prayer exercise or on a further explanation about some point of prayer.
* *Silent Prayer* (20 mins) based on the talk.
* *Guided review of the prayer time*. (5 mins) I usually ask some questions between pauses. These questions are to help the participants to notice what happened in the prayer, e.g. any difference in feelings between the beginning and ending of the prayer, any surprises, anything memorable, anything the participant wants to share? (see Chapter 6)
* *Sharing*. Usually in groups of three. (About 15 mins) (Chapter 13)
* *Suggestions* for praying until the next meeting.
* *Closing Prayer* by a member or a leader.
    (Some groups use music or relaxing exercises at the beginning. Tea is often served at the end or during the meeting.)

*Helping others to pray*
One of the aims of this book is to guide and encourage participants to help others to pray which, itself, is a great work. Besides that, experience teaches that the best way to learn and to come to understand anything is to try and explain it to others. So, helping others to pray better benefits the helper as well as the one helped. I have witnessed many examples of people who have started doing this. Some are now leaders of new groups; others help the old, the lonely, the hospitalised to pray better; still others have used parts of this book for teaching children in Sunday Schools, etc.

Many participants have gone on to attending individually directed retreats and to visiting regularly an experienced spiritual companion. I can see that, in the future, many lay-people in our churches will become such spiritual companions for others. I hope that this book will help this development.

*Teach from your own experience*
Throughout this book, I used stories from my own experience to explain things. I encourage leaders to use their own stories and experiences in a similar way rather than using mine. I hope this book may become a sample for some groups to prepare their own series of talks. Recently I heard from four ladies in Japan. They were veteran participants in this programme. They were preparing assiduously to start it in a neighbouring parish. They told me that after much reflection and discussion they had decided to begin from the exercises on praying nature. I was delighted to hear of their way of preparing and of their confidence in adjusting the content. I have since heard that the group is progressing wonderfully.

Also there are many, many other prayer exercises or ways of praying, e.g. using music, which are not included here. Likewise, while in this book we are not drawing on scripture or liturgy, participants may well feel drawn to a line in scripture that encapsulates points made here and inspires to deeper reflection. These are to be received with attention and gratitude.

So, happy and fruitful journeying to all of you who want to launch out into the deep!

# CHAPTER FIFTEEN

## *Background to this book and programme*

This book is the result of the efforts of many people. It is based on a book first published in Japanese in 2005. That, in turn, was based on talks in my own limited spoken Japanese, and on pages of my English notes translated into good Japanese, with great willingness and effort, by one of the participants. Many former participants helped in deciding what would be included and how it would be presented. Many hours of discussion went into the editing and printing of that book. I feel great gratitude and admiration towards so many.

Almost twenty years ago, I started a short course on prayer with some Japanese parishioners. I did so because, for a long time, I had felt the need for such a programme for people who had just been baptised and were adults. There were many programmes and books for leading people to baptism, but I could find nothing to help after they had been baptised. So finally I decided to start something myself and I soon found that many long-time baptised people also wanted to attend the course and wanted more help to pray better.

I started with only six talks, based on my own experiences in trying to pray better. The talks kept increasing. But I stuck to my resolve to talk only about what I had experienced and discovered by myself about prayer. My experience was enlarged by the input of many others. I went to talks and workshops on prayer. I did individually-directed retreats and sought personal spiritual guidance. I listened to tapes and read many books about praying and spiritual development. I kept trying to put what I was hearing into practice. I talked about what I was discovering.

I found that the more I tried to explain my experiences and discoveries to others, the more I myself deepened what I was learning. Also, listening to participants sharing about their own discoveries in prayer taught me a lot more.

In my second attempt, I announced I would start the prayer course for a year if there were 21 applicants. 63 applied. So I started three groups at once. At the end of each session, I gave out a printed summary of the talk. I also taped each session and left tapes of each talk in the office so that people could borrow them or copy them. Then I decided to divide the course into two parts, 'Praying as a Human' and 'Praying Scripture'.

Since then, I have conducted both courses many times but the course of 'Praying as a Human' has been the more frequent. Many of the same people continued to attend and repeat it again and again. Quite a few brought people from other churches and some of these started to lead this course in their own churches, using their experiences, the printouts and my tapes.

During the 16 years I was conducting these courses in Fujisawa, I was sick twice for two lengthy periods, but many of the participants formed groups and carried on without me. This gave me great satisfaction as well as gratitude to God and to them.

In my last two years, I decided I would do each of the courses one more time. I decided to do the 'Praying as a Human' course twice a month, on Saturdays. I announced that I was doing so in the hope that some men would attend because very few had ever attended, or could have, previously. I was hoping 10 or 12 might come. Then, some ladies, especially repeaters, asked could they attend and I agreed. To my amazement there were 106 applicants. So I had to make two big groups.

There were 17 men and of those 11 were doing it with their wives. One couple were catechumens, another couple were Protestant. There were three non-Christian husbands of former participants, a few Protestant women and a few non-Christian women. There were four Sisters and one Novice. A certain number were from churches outside Fujisawa. About 30 had done this course at least once before and they were a huge help in setting up the place, handling the printouts and name lists, keeping the sharing on the right lines, serving the tea, etc.

The next year I gave only the 'Praying Scripture' course while two teams of 'repeaters' conducted two courses of 'Praying as a Human'. I attended these but only as a participant – listening, praying and sharing with the others. I soon became convinced that the leaders explained and guided the courses better than I ever did. Their experiences as housewives, businessmen, office workers, parents, etc, in their own culture and in more natural language, gave more help to other participants than I could give. They planned a longer period for the course and moved more slowly. They started off by using my notes as well as their own experiences in prayer and in life. Gradually they talked more and more from their own experience. Two of the leaders of one group were businessmen who had been baptised less than ten years. Since I left last year, three new groups have started, one centring on couples. Another group has begun in a neighbouring parish.

Before I was scheduled to leave Japan I decided to arrange my material in folders for leaders of groups. I asked for feedback from former participants and we spent many hours in discussion. The outcome was that, instead of some folders, 1200 copies of a book were printed. 500 more copies have since been printed. So that is the background to this book which, with the help of many, many others, I am now presenting in English.

My dream is that the book will do more than help individuals to pray. I pray that it will stimulate new groups, learning from their own experiences and making useful adaptations, to guide others to pray better.

Recently I received this note from a young Japanese housewife and a leader of a new prayer group. I think it sums up so much of this book. She wrote, 'The Journey of Prayer? I am discovering that as long as I travel with the others, even an imperfect person like me can go it. My imperfections become the source of my strength.'